Wildlife Watching

Sea Turtle Watching

by Diane Bair and Pamela Wright

Consultant:
Daniel R. Evans
Coordinator, Sea Turtle Survival League
Caribbean Conservation Corporation

CAPSTONE BOOKS
an imprint of Capstone Press
Mankato, Minnesota

Capstone Books are published by Capstone Press
P.O. Box 669, 151 Good Counsel Drive, Mankato, Minnesota 56002
http://www.capstone-press.com

Library of Congress Cataloging-in-Publication Data
Bair, Diane.
    Sea turtle watching/Diane Bair and Pamela Wright.
    p. cm.—(Wildlife watching)
    Includes bibliographical references and index.
    Summary: Describes several species of sea turtles, their characteristics
and habitats, as well as places and techniques for safely observing these
endangered animals.
    ISBN 0-7368-0323-8
    1. Sea turtles—Juvenile literature. 2. Wildlife watching—Juvenile literature.
[1. Sea turtles. 2. Turtles. 3. Wildlife watching. 4. Endangered species.] I. Wright,
Pamela, 1953– . II. Title. III. Series: Bair, Diane. Wildlife watching.
QL666.C536B338 2000
597.92—DC21   99-25192
                                                   CIP

Editorial Credits

Carrie A. Braulick, editor; Steve Christensen, cover designer and illustrator;
    Heidi Schoof, photo researcher

Photo Credits

Ann Duncan/TOM STACK & ASSOCIATES, 33
Brian Parker/TOM STACK & ASSOCIATES, 24
Colephoto/Fred Whitehead, 19, 30
David B. Fleetham/TOM STACK & ASSOCIATES, 8, 42 (top)
David F. Clobes, cover inset, 16, 39
Doug Perrine/Innerspace Visions, cover, 28, 41 (top)
Hobe Sound Nature Center, 20
Index Stock Imagery, 40
James P. Rowan, 11
Jay Ireland and Georgienne Bradley, 45
Richard B. Levine, 13
Tammy Peluso/TOM STACK & ASSOCIATES, 4
Unicorn Stock Photos/Martin R. Jones, 37
Visuals Unlimited/Rick Poley, 14, 22; Marc Epstein, 34; Valorie Hodgson, 41 (bottom);
    Emily Stong, 42 (bottom)

**Thank you to Peter Lutz, Marine Biology, Florida Atlantic University, for his
assistance in preparing this book.**

Table of Contents

Chapter 1

Getting to Know Sea Turtles

Sea turtles are among the oldest living reptiles. Relatives of today's sea turtles were alive when dinosaurs lived on earth. Some sea turtle fossils are more than 150 million years old.

You can learn about these reptiles. You can find information about sea turtles in libraries and on the Internet. You may even be able to watch sea turtles.

About Sea Turtles

Seven species of sea turtles live in the world. Each type of sea turtle is called a species. Six

Sea turtles spend almost all of their time in the ocean.

sea turtle species live in oceans off coasts of North America. These include loggerhead, hawksbill, green, and leatherback sea turtles. Kemp's ridley and olive ridley sea turtles also live off North America's coast. Australian flatback sea turtles live only off Australia's northern coast.

Sea turtles are larger than turtles that live on land. Leatherbacks are the largest of all sea turtles. They also are the heaviest reptiles in the world. Leatherbacks can be 8 feet (2.4 meters) long and can weigh more than 1,000 pounds (454 kilograms). Kemp's ridleys and olive ridleys are the smallest sea turtles. These turtles usually are about 2 feet (.6 meter) long and weigh about 90 pounds (41 kilograms).

Sea turtles have four paddle-like limbs called flippers. Flippers help sea turtles quickly swim away from predators. Predators hunt other animals for food. Sea turtle predators include sharks and other large fish.

Sea Turtle Size Comparison

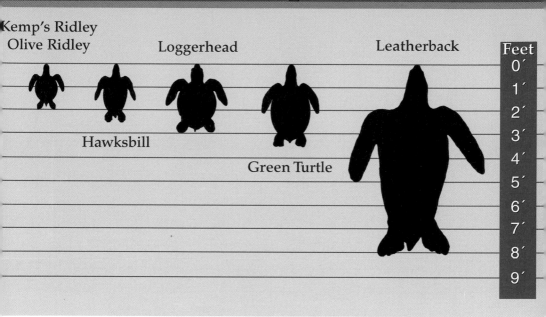

Kemp's Ridley
Olive Ridley
Loggerhead
Leatherback
Hawksbill
Green Turtle

Feet
0´
1´
2´
3´
4´
5´
6´
7´
8´
9´

Some sea turtles can swim as fast as 35 miles (56 kilometers) per hour. Sea turtles use their strong front flippers to push their bodies through the water. They use their back flippers to turn and to stop.

The Shell

Sea turtles have a shell made of bone. A sea turtle's shell is smooth, rounded, and

7

Most sea turtles have scutes on their shells.

streamlined. This helps sea turtles move easily
through water.

The top part of a sea turtle's shell is called a
carapace. A sea turtle's ribs and backbone are
attached to the carapace. Thin, flat pieces of
keratin called scutes cover the carapace of most
sea turtles. This strong material also makes up
people's fingernails. Leatherbacks are the only
sea turtles without scutes. These sea turtles have
a shell made of strong, rubbery skin.

A sea turtle's shell protects its inner body parts. But a sea turtle cannot protect its head by pulling it inside its shell like land turtles can.

Living Habits

Sea turtles eat a variety of food. They eat crabs, jellyfish, sea urchins, and fish. Sea turtles also eat algae. Algae are small plants that grow in water or damp places. Algae do not have roots, stems, leaves, or flowers. Most sea turtles have strong jaws and sharp beaks. This helps them crush their food.

Sea turtles must come to the water's surface to breathe air. They swim to the surface to breathe every few minutes when they are active. Sea turtles do not need to breathe air as often when they rest. They may stay underwater for many weeks during these times. Sea turtles sometimes rest at the bottom of the ocean. Female sea turtles often rest after they lay eggs.

Life Cycle of Sea Turtles

Sea turtles spend most of their lives in the ocean. They grow, eat, and mate in the water. But female sea turtles swim ashore to make nests and lay eggs. Most female sea turtles are at least 20 years old before they lay eggs.

Most female sea turtles lay eggs every two to three years. Kemp's and olive ridleys are the only sea turtles that lay eggs each year.

Sea turtles lay eggs during nesting season. This season is during spring and summer. Female sea turtles often lay their eggs on the same beaches where they hatched.

Sea turtles hatch from eggs after about 60 days. Young sea turtles are called hatchlings. Hatchlings rush to the ocean immediately after they hatch. Male sea turtles usually do not come ashore again after they enter the ocean.

Sea Turtles in Danger

Most sea turtles never reach adulthood. Scientists believe that only one out of 1,000 sea turtles lives long enough to mate. Some scientists believe the number of sea turtles has decreased by 50 percent during the last 20 years.

Hatchlings rush to the ocean immediately after they hatch.

All sea turtle species except loggerheads are endangered. Endangered sea turtles may soon die out. Loggerhead sea turtles are threatened. Threatened sea turtles may soon become endangered.

Sea turtles face many dangers. People are the biggest threat to sea turtles. For example, some people accidentally drive on sea turtle nests. This can kill the sea turtles in the nests. People who fish for shrimp may accidentally catch sea turtles in their nets. These people are called shrimpers. Sea turtles cannot escape from the nets to breathe.

People also destroy sea turtles' habitats. These are the natural places and conditions in which sea turtles live. They may pollute ocean water. They also may pollute ocean beaches. Wind or large waves can carry beach pollution into the water. Sea turtles may eat this trash. These sea turtles can die.

Some people build sea walls on beaches to prevent sand erosion near their property. Erosion occurs when ocean water washes sand away. But

People can help sea turtles by cleaning polluted beaches.

People sometimes place sea turtle eggs in hatcheries to keep them safe.

sea walls often block sea turtles' paths to suitable nesting areas. Sea turtles then may lay eggs in unsafe places.

Some people hunt sea turtles and their eggs. They may use sea turtles and their eggs for food. They also may use sea turtles to make various products. People sometimes use sea turtle skin to make leather. They may use sea turtle shells for jewelry.

Predators also threaten sea turtle populations. Raccoons, crabs, and foxes eat sea turtle eggs. Sea birds eat hatchlings on beaches. A variety of predators eat hatchlings in the ocean.

Protecting Sea Turtles

Some countries have laws that protect sea turtles. It is illegal throughout the world to sell sea turtles and sea turtle products between countries. In the United States, it is illegal to harm, disturb, or kill sea turtles or their eggs. All shrimpers in the United States are required to put turtle excluder devices in their nets. These special boxes allow sea turtles to escape from shrimp nets.

People who live near sea turtles may keep their outside lights dim or off. Hatchlings look for moonlight reflected off the water to locate the ocean. Other light can cause them to go in the wrong direction.

Sea turtle conservation groups work to protect sea turtles. People in these groups may teach others about dangers sea turtles face. Some build sea turtle hatcheries. People move sea turtle eggs to these places if sea turtles' natural nesting areas are unsafe.

Chapter 2

Preparing for Your Adventure

You should only go on guided programs to observe sea turtles. These programs often are called turtle walks. Guides on turtle walks make sure sea turtles are not disturbed. You may disturb sea turtles if you look for them on your own. Nesting sea turtles that are disturbed may stop laying eggs and return to the ocean.

Learn as much as you can about sea turtles before you go on turtle walks. Check out sea turtle books from libraries. You may want to look for sea turtle web sites on the Internet.

You can learn about sea turtles on the Internet.

Learning about Turtle Walks

Members of sea turtle conservation groups sometimes organize turtle walks. People who live near sea turtles' nesting areas also may help organize these walks.

Guides take several actions to make sure sea turtles are not disturbed. They make sure visitors stay a safe distance from sea turtles. They also make sure visitors do not handle sea turtles.

Most turtle walks are conducted for visitors to see loggerhead sea turtles. All other sea turtle species are endangered. Endangered sea turtles should be left completely undisturbed to increase their chances of survival.

Several sources provide information about turtle walks. You can contact places in coastal areas that offer turtle walks. Some of these places are listed under "Places to See Sea Turtles" on page 26 of this book. Workers at these places can tell you when turtle walks are planned.

You usually will see only loggerhead sea turtles on turtle walks.

You also can use the Internet to learn about turtle walks. Search for web sites of cities located near the ocean. These web sites often contain information about nearby activities. Some web sites may have information about turtle walks.

Turtle walks are conducted at night.

When to Go

People usually conduct turtle walks between
June and August. Most sea turtles lay eggs
during this time. Turtle walks usually are
conducted at night. Sea turtles usually lay their
eggs during the night. Sea turtles often hatch
during the coolest part of the night. This is
usually between 11 p.m. and midnight. Visitors
have a better chance of seeing sea turtles during
these times.

What to Bring

Some items may be useful on turtle walks. Bring a sweater or a light jacket. You may want a blanket. Summer nights often are cool. Bring insect repellent. This will help protect you from insect bites.

You may have to wait for a sea turtle to come into view. You may want to bring a bottle of water and a snack. Be sure to dispose of garbage properly. This helps protect the land and water from pollution.

Do not bring a flashlight on turtle walks. Light from flashlights may confuse hatchlings. They then may get lost on their way to the ocean. Light from flashlights also may affect female sea turtles. Female sea turtles may not come ashore to lay eggs if they see bright lights.

Turtle walk guides often have a flashlight covered with a piece of red cellophane. People often use this thin, clear material to wrap items. The red cellophane makes the beams of light look red. Sea turtles cannot see red very well. These red beams are less likely to bother sea turtles.

Do not bring a camera on turtle walks. Light from a camera's flash also may disturb sea turtles.

Chapter 3

Where to Look

Observe sea turtles at their nesting beaches. Some wildlife refuges or state and national parks have sea turtle nesting beaches. You also may observe sea turtles at vacation resorts or near marine science centers.

Nesting Beaches

Many sea turtles nest on beaches of the southeastern United States. Most of these beaches are south of the state of North Carolina. They also nest on beaches of Puerto Rico, Hawaii, and the U.S. Virgin Islands.

Different sea turtle species nest in different areas. Hawksbill sea turtles nest on beaches throughout the Caribbean Sea. They rarely nest

You may see hatchlings enter the ocean on nesting beaches.

Different sea turtle species have different nesting beaches.

on North American coasts. Leatherbacks often nest on the northern coast of South America.

Turtle Walks at Nesting Beaches

You may go on a turtle walk and not see any sea turtles. Guides cannot predict exactly when sea turtles will lay eggs. They also do not know exactly when sea turtles will hatch.

But you still can learn about sea turtles on these walks.

Some people who run turtle walks conduct sea turtle presentations. At these presentations, you may listen to talks or watch videos about sea turtles. Guides also can teach you about sea turtles during turtle walks.

You should make reservations before you go on turtle walks. Reservations will save a place for you on the walks. Many people may want to go on turtle walks. But groups on turtle walks are small. Most groups include fewer than 30 people. Large groups may disturb sea turtles.

Places to See Sea Turtles

1 **Bald Head Island,**
near Wilmington, North Carolina:
About one hundred loggerhead nests can be found here each year.
The Bald Head Island Conservancy conducts turtle walks from
mid-June to mid-August.

2 **Hobe Sound National Wildlife Refuge,**
Jupiter Island, Florida:
People have recorded more than 1,000 loggerhead nests at this
refuge. Green and leatherback sea turtles sometimes nest here. The
Hobe Sound Nature Center runs turtle walks during June and July.

3 **Jekyll Island,**
near Brunswick, Georgia:
About 100 loggerhead sea turtle nests are located on this
island each year. Volunteers conduct turtle walks from June
through August.

4 **John D. MacArthur Beach State Park,**
North Palm Beach, Florida:
This beach usually has more than 1,000 loggerhead sea turtle nests
each year. Green and leatherback sea turtles also sometimes nest on
this beach. The park's nature center offers turtle walks during June
and July.

5 **Sebastian Inlet State Recreation Area,**
Melbourne Beach, Florida:
About 1,000 loggerhead turtle nests can be found in this area each
year. Turtle walks are conducted during June and July.

6 **Museum of Discovery and Science,**
Fort Lauderdale, Florida:
This museum offers sea turtle walks during June and July. A live
nest of loggerhead sea turtle eggs is on display during summer.

Chapter 4

Making Observations

You can make many observations on turtle walks. You may observe sea turtle eggs or tracks. You may watch hatchlings emerge. You then can record these observations.

Sea Turtle Nesting

You may watch sea turtles make nests. Nesting sea turtles follow several steps. They first use their flippers to dig a body pit. Sea turtles next dig an egg chamber with their hind flippers. Loggerhead egg chambers usually are about 3 feet (.9 meter) deep and less than one foot (.3 meter) wide.

You may see sea turtles make their nests while you are on a turtle walk.

Sea turtles lay their eggs in the chamber. They usually lay two or three eggs at a time. Some sea turtles lay more than 100 eggs. These white, round eggs look like ping pong balls. Sea turtle eggs are flexible. They do not break when sea turtles drop them into the chamber.

Never touch or handle sea turtle eggs. Sea turtle eggs are strong, but you still can harm them.

You may see nesting sea turtles release water from their eyes. Scientists believe this helps rid their bodies of salt from ocean water. Salt collects in sea turtles' bodies when they eat ocean plants and animals. Too much salt is not healthy for sea turtles.

Sea turtles use their flippers to fill the pit with sand after they lay eggs. They cover their body pit to hide it from predators. Sea turtles may take one to three hours to finish nesting.

Sea turtles return to the ocean after they lay eggs. The hot, damp sand keeps the eggs warm. This warmth helps the sea turtles hatch. Female sea turtles do not return to the beach until it is

Sea turtle eggs are white, round, and flexible.

time to lay eggs again. Some sea turtles lay eggs four or five times during one nesting season.

Sea Turtle Hatchlings

Most sea turtles hatch in late summer. They hatch from eggs underground. Sea turtles then crawl up through the sand. Most hatchlings are 1 to 2 inches (2.5 to 5 centimeters) long.

Guides may put a stethoscope on the nests during turtle walks to find out if the turtles are hatching. A doctor or nurse uses this listening device to listen to a patient's heart and lungs. Guides use stethoscopes to listen for sea turtles moving through the sand. This makes a sound similar to rushing water. Sometimes you can hear this sound without a stethoscope. To listen, put your ear next to the sand. But do not do this unless a guide gives you permission.

Sea turtle walk guides sometimes keep in touch with each other by radio. They may tell each other when sea turtles hatch. The turtle walk groups then meet to watch the turtles hatch.

Hatchlings climb up through the sand after they hatch.

To the Ocean

You may notice that sea turtle hatchlings do not move toward the ocean in an orderly way. You may see some go the wrong way and then turn around. You may see hatchlings go back toward the nest.

Do not disturb or touch hatchlings as they move toward the ocean. Hatchlings are very small. You may harm them. Do not step on hatchlings. Stand still until all of the turtles enter the ocean.

Sea Turtle Tracks

Look for sea turtle tracks on turtle walks. Sea turtles make wavy ridges in the sand as they drag themselves across the beach. The tracks often lead to sea turtles' nests.

Do not disturb sea turtle tracks. Other people may follow the tracks to nests. They may want to move the eggs to a hatchery or another safe place on the beach.

You may observe sea turtle tracks on turtle walks.

Protected Nests

You may see hatcheries or other protected nesting areas as you walk along a beach. You may see marked or numbered sea turtle nests. Members of sea turtle conservation groups may mark or number nests to keep track of them.

People protect nests in various ways. They sometimes put metal screens over or around sea turtle nests. This keeps the eggs safe from predators. They may put signs up near sea turtle nests. These signs inform other people where sea turtle nests are located.

Recording Your Observations

You may want to record your sea turtle observations. It may be hard to take notes about sea turtles at night. Observe sea turtles as carefully as possible at night. Record your observations in the morning.

You may record many sea turtle observations. Record sea turtles' sizes. Keep track of the time it took sea turtles to complete

You may see marked sea turtle nests on turtle walks.

each step of nesting. Write down how sea turtle eggs looked. Note if the sea turtles were releasing water from their eyes. Write down about how many hatchlings you saw. Describe how the hatchlings moved into the ocean.

You may want to draw pictures or take photographs after you go on turtle walks. You can draw a picture of the sea turtle nests or hatchlings. You may want to photograph sea turtle tracks.

You may not observe sea turtles on some turtle walks. But you still can note what you learned about sea turtles from guides. You may learn about sea turtles' nesting habits. You also can learn about different sea turtle species.

You may want to teach others about your sea turtle watching experiences. This can help people understand sea turtles. People who learn about sea turtles may want to protect these animals. This can help sea turtles survive for many more years.

Record your sea turtle observations in the morning.

Loggerhead Sea Turtle

Description: Loggerheads are the most common sea turtles. These sea turtles are about 3 feet (.9 meter) long. They usually weigh 150 to 350 pounds (68 to 159 kilograms). Loggerheads get their name because they have large heads compared to other sea turtles. Their heads may be 10 inches (25 centimeters) wide. Loggerheads have red-brown shells. The top and sides of their heads have yellow borders. Their necks and shoulders are brown on top and yellow on the sides and bottom. The underside of loggerhead shells also are yellow. Loggerheads have powerful jaws to crush their food.

Loggerheads lay eggs about every two or three years. About 50,000 to 70,000 loggerhead nests are located in the United States each year. Most of these nests are on Florida's coast. Loggerheads are the only sea turtles that are threatened. All other sea turtle species are endangered.

Habitat: Shallow water near continental coasts, bays, and river openings

Food: Crabs, mollusks, clams, sponges

The loggerhead turtle is the state reptile of South Carolina. Large numbers of these turtles nest in this state.

Leatherback Sea Turtle

Description: Leatherbacks are the largest of all
sea turtles. They usually are 4 to 8 feet (1.2 to
2.4 meters) long. They usually weigh 650 to
1,300 pounds (295 to 590 kilograms). The largest
leatherback ever recorded weighed more than
2,000 pounds (907 kilograms). Leatherbacks
have strong, rubbery shells with seven long
ridges. The ridges usually are black with white
spots. Leatherbacks travel greater distances than
any other sea turtle. They also make the deepest
dives. Leatherbacks can dive as deep as 3,000
feet (914 meters). Leatherbacks sometimes nest
on the coasts of the U.S. Virgin Islands
and Florida.

Habitat: Deep ocean water, often live in
cold water

Food: Jellyfish

Green Sea Turtle

Description: Green sea turtles are about 3.5 feet
(1 meter) long and weigh about 300 pounds
(136 kilograms). Green sea turtles have dark
brown shells. They are named for the green
color of their body fat. Green sea turtles have
smaller heads than other sea turtles in relation
to their body size. Adult green turtles have
different diets than other adult sea turtles. Adult
green sea turtles eat only plants. Young green
sea turtles and all other adult sea turtles
sometimes eat other animals. Some green
turtles nest on Florida's coast and the
Hawaiian islands.

Habitat: Bays, near continental
coasts and islands

Food: Sea grass, algae

Hawksbill Sea Turtle

Description: Hawksbill sea turtles are about
2.5 feet (.8 meter) long. They usually weigh 100
to 150 pounds (45 to 68 kilograms). Hawksbills
are named for their beak-like upper jaws. Their
shells have thick, overlapping scutes. Some
people kill hawksbill sea turtles for their shells.
They often use the shells to make jewelry.
Hawksbills are slow swimmers compared to
most other sea turtles. Hawksbills usually swim
about 11 miles (18 kilometers) per day. Most
other sea turtle species swim about 15 to 56
miles (24 to 90 kilometers) per day. Hawksbills
nest on beaches of the Caribbean Sea. They
rarely nest on North American coasts.

Habitat: Shallow water near sandy and rocky
areas, near river openings

Food: Sponges, fish, sea anemones, shrimp

Kemp's Ridley Sea Turtle

Description: Kemp's ridleys are the rarest of all
sea turtles. They usually are 1 to 2 feet (.3 to .6
meter) long. They weigh about 100 pounds
(45 kilograms). Kemp's ridleys have olive-green
or gray shells. Today, there are fewer than 500
nesting Kemp's ridleys. These sea turtles often
die when they are trapped in shrimp and fishing
nets. Female Kemp's ridleys nest in groups.
Most Kemp's ridleys nest in Mexico. They
sometimes nest on Padre Island in Texas.

Habitat: Shallow areas with sandy bottoms

Food: Crabs, clams, mussels, shrimp, fish, sea
urchins, squid, jellyfish

Words to Know

algae (AL-jee)—small plants that grow in water or on damp surfaces; algae do not have roots, stems, leaves, or flowers.

carapace (KAR-uh-payss)—the top part of a sea turtle's shell

erosion (i-ROH-zhuhn)—loss of sand caused by the wearing away of beaches by water

hatchling (HACH-ling)—a sea turtle that has recently hatched

migrate (MYE-grate)—to move from one area to another as the seasons change

predator (PRED-uh-tur)—an animal that hunts other animals for food

scute (SKOOT)—a thin, flat piece of keratin on a sea turtle's shell

turtle excluder device (TUR-tuhl ek-SKLOOD-ur di-VISSE)—a special box shrimpers use that allows sea turtles to escape from shrimp nets

To Learn More

Cerulean, Susan and Ann Morrow. *Florida Wildlife Viewing Guide.* The Watchable Wildlife Series. Helena, Mont.: Falcon Press, 1998.

Gibbons, Gail. *Sea Turtles.* New York: Holiday House, 1995.

O'Keefe, M. Timothy. *Sea Turtles: The Watcher's Guide.* Lakeland, Fla.: Larsen's Outdoor Publishing, 1995.

Patton, Don. *Sea Turtles.* Plymouth, Minn.: Child's World, 1996.

Ripple, Jeff. *Sea Turtles.* World Life Library. Stillwater, Minn.: Voyageur Press, 1996.

Useful Addresses

Archie Carr Center for Sea Turtle Research
Bartram Hall
P.O. Box 118525
University of Florida
Gainesville, FL 32611

Caribbean Conservation Corporation
4424 13th Street NW
Suite A1
Gainesville, FL 32609

World Wildlife Fund—Canada
245 Eglinton Avenue East
Suite 410
Toronto, ON M4P 3J1
Canada

Internet Sites

Caribbean Conservation Corporation
http://cccturtle.org

National Marine Fisheries Service
http://www.nmfs.gov/prot_res/turtles/
   turtle.html

Turtle Time, Inc.
http://www.swflorida.com/turtletime

Turtle Trax
http://www.turtles.org

U.S. Fish and Wildlife Service Kid's Corner
   http://www.fws.gov/r9endspp/kid_cor/
   kid_cor.htm

Index